THE DAY MY SOUL CRIED

A Memoir by Yvonne N. Pierre

THE DAY MY SOUL CRIED

THE DAY MY SOUL CRIED: A MEMOIR

ISBN 10: 0615354971

ISBN 13: 978-0-615-35497-2

Written by Yvonne N. Pierre

Edited by Ann K. Fisher

Cover and interior designs by Yvonne N. Pierre

Sketch of woman by Jeffrey R. Miller

Website: http://www.zyonair.com

Published by Zyonair's Unlimited, LLC, Marietta, GA 30062

THE DAY MY SOUL CRIED

TABLE OF CONTENTS

phases

THE DAY MY SOUL CRIED

INTRODUCTION

*T*he *Day My Soul Cried* is a memoir that takes you on a journey from Yvonne Pierre's childhood to adulthood and the many obstacles encountered along the way. The book is divided into different phases that led her to the day her soul cried; from the time her spirit was broken to when it was unbroken and the lessons learned along the way.

THE DAY MY SOUL CRIED

BROKEN

Some of the greatest battles will be fought within the silent chambers of your own soul.

- E. T. Benson

THE DAY MY SOUL CRIED

BROKEN

It's amazing how the world looks through the eyes of a small child. I can remember as far back as too short to reach the top of the kitchen sink. Everything seemed so big around me. But life was grand, no worries, little responsibility (except cleaning up behind myself), and no stress; playing hopscotch, jump rope, racing to the stop light, mud pies, and laughing. My God, those were the days! I would try to play as much as I could before it was time to go home and that was when the street lights came on. How I wanted to hold on to every moment. I used to beg my mother, "Please, please, oh mom please, just a few more minutes."

But as we get older, we tend to see the world differently. Things happen in our lives that alter how we view the world, ourselves, and others. I loved being under my mom. I never wanted her to leave. I remember feeling saddened when she said the words, "Okay girls, be good, I'll be back... I love you." Sometimes I would hide when it was time for her to go, hoping that would keep her home. I thought that if she couldn't tell me she was leaving, she wouldn't leave. That didn't work, of course, but I tried. I enjoyed watching her laugh when we would watch TV, or when we did something funny. I wanted her so badly to be happy, because even at a young age, I knew she wasn't.

When it was time for bed, I would gaze out the window in amazement of everything and I used to think, "Wow, how is this all possible?" I appreciated the little things, like my mom tucking me and my sister in at night, spending the night at grandma's house, birthday parties, family gathering, school events, field trips, playing – I could go on and on. If we couldn't go outside, my sister and I would get anything that looked like a microphone and just sing and dance.

It seemed like every week we were going to someone's birthday party and we spent a lot of time with our cousins. Mom would occasionally take us to the movies, out to eat, and visiting with her friends and family. Oh, I almost forgot to mention, my sister and I were Brownies in the Girl Scouts and Mom was our troop leader. That was so much fun, too.

Aside from playing from sun-up to sundown, it seemed like we were ALWAYS at church with our grandmother. OMG, there was so much shouting, crying, and singing. I had no idea why so many tears, but I always looked forward to going. Well, not for the shouting and crying; I looked forward to my grandma giving me a dollar to put in church and 50 cents for the candy store on the corner, and playing with our church friends. That's what we called them because that was the only time we saw that group of friends, at church. It was a small church, maybe 20 to 30 members on a good day. I think everyone in the church was related in some way, except for us. My sister and I sung in the choir, well kinda. Okay, I wasn't much of a singer, but I loved singing in the choir. They would give us a music sheet with the words to practice, but I couldn't read it. I shamelessly admit that I did a lot of lip synching. During church, when the pastor would give her sermon, although I had no clue what she was talking about, I assumed it must have been very important, because I would get in trouble for falling asleep. Well, I guess my loud snoring did not help. My grandmother would nudge me and give me "the look." I knew I'd better straight up.

There was one thing in the pastors' sermon that was very clearly understood, and that was if I was bad, I was going to hell and if I'm good I'll go to heaven. I didn't quite understand what hell was, but I knew it was hot and a place I surely did not want to go.

Oh my goodness, nicknames. Most of my peers had cute nicknames. Ha! Oh no, not me. My nickname was MOTOR MOUTH. I don't know who came up with it; I think it might have been my mom. I guess the name came from the fact that I talked nonstop. I got into trouble a lot for talking at school. From the time I woke up until the time I went to bed my mouth was moving. Most of what was coming out of my mouth were questions. My goodness, I had so many questions about everything – why, why, why? For every answer, I had one or two more questions. For example, you couldn't just tell me the moon and the stars were in the sky. I would ask, well, what's beyond that? Where does it end? If it don't end, how is that possible? Ha! It's funny; I asked so many questions I was put out of children's Bible class.

Of all the questions, there were some I guess I never thought to ask. I remember I was playing with this little girl, I don't remember her name or face, but I do remember her question, "Where is your daddy?" I had never thought about it before that moment. Without thinking, I just said, "I don't have one." She said, "Everyone has a daddy!" I never questioned it, because I thought it was normal for it to be just my sister, mom, grandma, and me. It's funny; I didn't notice everyone had a daddy until then. It seemed like after that everywhere I looked I saw kids with their fathers. I started to wonder: Why does everyone have a daddy but me. Where is my daddy?

I don't remember how my mom explained it but she told me my father was deceased. I had no earthly idea what deceased meant. I'm sure she explained it but I did not understand. However, now I had an answer for the next time someone asked me where my father was. I would proudly say, "Oh, he's deceased." My father's mother name was Yvonne and I was named after her.

We would talk to her often. She would send gifts for holidays and would telephone frequently. She would send pictures and write long heartfelt letters. We called her Grandma Vonn. Grandma Vonn sent us a photo of our daddy and I would just stare at his picture. Although, I still did not fully understand, I knew I would never get to see him. I heard he was a good father. It wasn't until I was old enough to understand that it was explained to me that he was murdered. I was about ten years old and I asked my mom what happened to my father. She told me we were home all day with him. She was at work and when she got home from work they got into an argument. He got upset and left out the house. He went to a bar with his friend for a few drinks. Hours later, the police came to the door and told my mom they believed her husband was killed and she needed to identify his body. He was shot in the back at a local bar and when he was brought to the hospital he was dead on arrival. My mom had now lost her father, her husband, and her grandfather all within two years. I could see the pain in her eyes as she talked about it. I did not ask many questions, but I could tell it was very hard on her. I didn't like seeing my mom in pain. We both started to cry and she grabbed me and it seemed like we hugged for hours.

I was too young to remember my father; I think I was about two or three years old when he died so horribly. But I missed him so much. All of my friends had both of their parents at home and I began to yearn for that. I became very angry that someone took him away from me. I was so mad that I never got to know him or experience having someone to call dad. I just wanted a chance to hug him and for him to tuck me in at night. Since, I never experienced it, it made me feel so incomplete. Those who knew him often told me that I looked just like him. I would just stare at his picture and wonder what life would be like if he were here. Sometimes I would catch my mom looking at me and I could feel she was missing my dad. I remember staring out the window; I guess I was about seven, crying myself to sleep. God, why? How could someone take him away from my sister and me? How could someone leave my mom in so much pain? I started slowly seeing the world differently.

I don't remember when the nightmares started, but I don't remember never having them. It was a recurring nightmare of demons and monsters trying to attack me. I would always hide in the closet, but knew that wherever I ran I wasn't safe. I had gotten to the point where I could control when I woke up. But, no matter what I did the nightmares would not stop. I would wake myself up and run into my mom's bedroom.

Years later…

A lot happened over the next few years, both good and bad. We had moved in and out of grandma's house. My mom had a son. My little brother was born when I was ten. I had gone out of town on field trips with the school – Disneyworld and to The White House. My grandmother and mother would alternate each year on which one of us was going, because they could not afford to send both of us. Except for Disneyworld – grandma, my cousin, sister, and I all went on this trip. I wasn't the perfect little angel, oh the whippings. I was a runner, when momma got the belt, I got to running. I knew I would get caught eventually, but I needed time to prepare for it. I got many spankings, or should I say beatings and punishment.

It's amazing how the mind works. As a child, I held onto the good times, until my perception of this simple life changed. There are moments, small fractions of our life that change our views almost instantly. When I was about twelve years old, in the seventh grade, and in one particular class, on Fridays, we would watch educational movies that applied to what we were learning in class. I don't remember the class, why we were watching the film, or even the name of it, but just a few moments of the film changed my life. This film triggered memories of my childhood when my innocence was taken.

It was time to watch the movie. The teacher turned the lights off and gestured to the student aide to start the film. About ten minutes into watching it, the tears began to fall. My chest was hurting so bad, and it felt like I had cotton in my throat. I started tapping my foot and wiggling in my chair to make it look like I had to go to the bathroom. I needed to escape. I frantically asked the teacher if I could go to the bathroom and I hid my face. I wanted to run and scream. I ran into the bathroom and locked the door. I had a blank look on my face as the tears continued to roll. I was in shock, confused, and my heart felt like it was going to beat through my chest. The girl in the movie had been molested as a child. I didn't even know what molested was until that moment.

Flashback…

When I was little, we had many babysitters. For the most part, we had a lot of fun. Many of them had children our age, except for one family friend who would often take care of us. She had adult sons – I don't remember how many, but it was a large family. Two of her sons molested me; one was in his 30s and the other was in his 20s. The eldest of the two, his name was Junior, molested me on a regular basis. I don't remember when I became his "secret wife." I was only about five when it started. I was a baby. You see, I thought I was doing what I was supposed to do as his "girlfriend," but no one could know about this secret. When I would slip and tell people he was my boyfriend, they thought, I was just a kid with a crush. I remember part of my duties was to watch him use the bathroom, oral sex, and assist in masturbation. He would fondle me. I had to sit in the corner between the wall and toilet to watch him. He wasn't our babysitter, well, not at first;

his mom was. But when she had something to do, she would have Junior, who lived with her, take care of us. Often we would spend the night. When Junior's mom and everyone else in the house would go to sleep, he would wake me up to come get in the bed with him. Some of this memory is blurry. I remember he would wait until my sister went to sleep and I asked him why not my sister? He told me because I was the prettiest. He used to tell me that when I get older he was going to marry me and that he loved me.

This went on for years. I remember he had moved out and had gotten married. I did not understand it then, but I was so angry, thinking he had promised to marry me. His wife and others were around when I started yelling, "You were supposed to marry me!" I was only eight or nine at the time. No one had any idea what was wrong with me, or why I was so mad. They thought it was because I had an innocent crush on him. I never saw him or his family again.

Back in the bathroom at school...

When all this and more flashed through my head, I became devastated, mad, and so hurt. I was afraid to tell my mother. I did not want to disappoint her. It was my fault. All these memories flashed before my eyes. I thought it was my entire fault. Entirely my fault. How could I allow this to happen? When I got home that day, I could not wait to take a bath. I ran the water as hot as I could and tried to wash off the hurt and shame. I was screaming on the inside.

I did not want to go to church anymore. I was bound for hell and questioned God. How could there be a God? Why didn't He protect me? Why did God take my father? This wouldn't have happened if my father was here to protect me. Then I started questioning myself. I believed I brought this on myself. How could I have let this continue?

This started me on a self-destructive path.

THE ESCAPE

*Life's challenges are not supposed to paralyze you;
they're supposed to help you discover who you are.*

- B. J. Reagon

THE DAY MY SOUL CRIED

THE ESCAPE

By the time I was twelve years old, my future was the last thing on my mind, if at all. Many preteens talked about what they wanted to be when they grew up. Not me; I was trying *not* to think about it.

While others my age were daydreaming about their future, all I cared about was planning what I was going to drink, where I was going to smoke, and how I was going to sneak away to have sex with my boyfriend, who was a couple years older. My concern was saving up my lunch money to chip in on getting high for that day. While everyone was planning what they were going to wear to school, I was questioning where I was going to hangout until school was over. I didn't care where, anywhere but in class.

You see, I had given up on the idea that there was a chance for me to get it right. I had given up that I had a future, so why prepare for what I thought wouldn't happen anyway? I was damaged goods. I just wanted the emptiness, pain, shame, and embarrassment to go away. I wanted to be NUMB. The more I tried to escape, the more pain I brought on myself and those who loved me, but I didn't see it that way.

School was a battle of its own. In high school, I had to go to summer school and night school every year just to get to the next grade. My mom spent a lot of time and money on tutors, but I just wasn't getting it. Why can't I get this? What is wrong with me? I would hear the kids laughing when I get stuck on words, never knowing the right answer to the teachers' questions. And going up to the black board was torture. I was pretty good in math, but I would play it safe and request basic math classes. But English and History, oh my God, get me out of here. I needed to escape. I guess I did have a dream for myself and that was to have the power to disappear or simply fly away. Not forever, just in certain situations, like being in class.

While others were picking on the smart kids and calling them nerds, I wished I was one of them. I used to wish I could just answer the questions right. I used to wish that all I had to do was study before class. I wondered how other kids knew answers. I used to think it was something special they possessed. Someone told me, "Just study." Hah! I wished it was that simple for me. Study something I don't understand? Right! I lost hope in my ability to learn.

I just wanted to be able to read without getting stuck on words. Without having someone to tell me what every other word in a paragraph was. The teachers used to assign paragraphs in the book to each student. Some teachers based this on where you were seated. I would count to see which paragraph I would have to read and study it before it was my turn. Occasionally, they would switch up. I remember I was ready with my short paragraph and asked the child next to me to help me pronounce the words I had a hard time with. I would read it over and over. It was almost my turn. I was next.

The teacher told the student in front of me, "You read that well. Since the next paragraph is short, go ahead and read that one too." I panicked. The next one was very long and I hadn't studied it. I started planning my getaway. I had to get out of this class. I would play sick, go to the bathroom, or have to do something to get me out of the classroom, but I couldn't escape; I struggled my way through it and was humiliated.

I have no idea why some of my peers skipped school, but for me it was to avoid embarrassment. I would walk in the front door when my grandmother dropped me off at school, put my books in my locker and walk back out the back door. There was always somewhere to go and drink and get high until time to go home. On the days when there was no skipping spot available, I would just sit in the school bathroom until lunch hour. Then, I knew I only had a few more hours to hide out until it was time to go home.

I knew I could not get a job when I graduated, that is, if I graduated. I had a "D" average. I did just enough to get by. Eventually, everything started to catch up with me. I got suspended on what's called "Title 20." You have to go to a hearing and a board has to determine if and when you can come back to school. All the fighting, skipping, and getting into trouble at school led me to getting banned from all Gary, Indiana public schools. At the hearing, some people had disgust on their faces and others looked saddened. One of them grabbed my record, which was as thick as a 150-page book. She looked at me and said, "You are a disgrace to your mother, yourself, and this school. You are a menace and you do not belong with other students who want to learn." Believe it or not, I was devastated. You see, I saw myself as a victim, so I did not see this as something I brought on myself. I was sent to an alternative school. Alternative school is an adult education school that offers individuals an opportunity to receive their GED or high school diploma. Again, I can see the expressions on my mother and grandmother's faces; they were so upset and disappointed in me. I was breaking their hearts. But they never stopped trying to save me from myself. True, I did not agree, and still don't agree, with their tactics, but they did not give up. I was completely out of control. No matter what tactics they tried, as a "victim" I did not see it as this is punishment I deserve. Whippings, I would run or run away. Punishment, I would wait for my mother to go to sleep and sneak out. She sent my sister and me to jail, well, to a juvenile detention center. I got worse when I got out. You see, in my mind I was a victim so everything they did to stop me, I saw as their being against me, too.

And boys and dating shouldn't have been my focus either, like everything else I did at that age. Believe it or not, I still had some respect for myself, as far as boyfriends went.

Since, I had abandonment issues, I was very cautious about who I allowed near my heart. I had rules to protect my heart. Although sex should not have been on my mind when I was sixteen, I had a 30-to-90 day rule. If he is still interested after 30 to 90 days of talking, then I would consider giving him "some." Not realizing that every time, I was giving away a piece of my soul. The 30-to-90 day rule was based on how much I liked them. One guy, who I liked a lot, I had reservations about for various reasons. One reason was because I heard he was dating someone else. Let's just call him Robert. Robert and I decided to just be friends.

We were close friends, I thought. I started dating another guy at the time, let's just call him Mark.

Robert went to the alternative school and would take me home occasionally. That was my boy; I thought we were cool. One day, Robert asked me to ride with him – we were going to get some lunch. On the way, he said he had to make a stop at home. I thought nothing of it. I stayed in the car. He yelled out to the car and asked me to come in; he said it was taking longer than he thought. I still thought nothing of it. The thought of dating him repulsed me. We.re just friends, I believed.

When I got in the house, he became very aggressive. I thought I knew him, but when I looked in his eyes it was like the person I knew wasn't there. He pushed me down, ripped my clothing off, and I fought back. He hit me and called me a bitch. I stopped fighting when I saw his face – he looked demonic. I started to cry and begged him to stop. He overpowered me. He told me this was what I wanted. The tears started to stream down my face as I felt like my soul was leaving my body. What have I done? Why is this happening to me? I brought this on myself, I thought. I feared for my life and I just played it cool for my own safety. I just wanted to get home.

He did not take me home. He took me back to the school. Well, not exactly back to school. He kicked me out of the car blocks away from the school. He said, "Bitch, get the fuck out of my car." I did not argue with him, I just got out of the car. What the hell just happened? I was in shock; I was scared, confused, and numb. I just started walking, no plan on how I was going to get home. And I was blank.

People feared and respected Robert, so who was I going to tell? I told one person who I thought was my friend. She laughed and told me that I better not tell anyone. I was told I was a liar and that I asked for it. "Do you know what they do to a rapist in prison? Why would you do that to him? Don't be selfish; that was not rape," this so-called friend said. Wow! Again with a blank look on my face, I walked away as she kept talking. I questioned our entire friendship. Needless to say, that friendship faded very fast after that. I felt betrayed. Although this was the late '80s, things were still hush-hush and stuff like that wasn't openly talked about.

I didn't tell, Mark, the guy I was dating at the time. I thought two things would have happened: he would blame me, too, or he might try to hurt Robert. So, I just kept it to myself and tried to go on as if it never happened.

Gin and vodka became my best friends. Naturally, the drinking got very out of hand. At 17 years old, I had to drink to be sober. I could not function without alcohol in my system. I drank a half pint of gin when I woke up in the morning. I only went to school because I had to. It wasn't an option in my house. But I would just go to fill a seat. I felt like there was no place in this world for me, I was damaged goods and hell bound. Every guy I dated during this time, cheated. The guys who that cared about me, I pushed away. I was always looking for the other shoe to drop. I would get into relationships that I knew wouldn't work, to prevent myself from getting hurt. Right, that didn't work. I would still get hurt. I had to protect my heart. I expected the worse. Although, deep down inside, I wanted it, I was afraid of love. I became a runner. If I felt myself getting too close, I would do something to sabotage the relationship and move on. Eventually, I mastered how to turn my feelings on and off.

THE AWAKENING

The difficulties of life are intended to make us better, not bitter.

- Unknown

THE DAY MY SOUL CRIED

THE AWAKENING

There are times in our lives where we are forced to pay attention to our actions. I did not realize what I was doing to myself, let alone my mother and grandmother.

I lived for the day; I wasn't too concerned with the consequences of my actions that I would have to face in the future. One party after another and nothing else mattered; well at least that's what I told myself. There was something outside of my control always trying to get my attention. There were many wake-up calls, and the more I tried to ignore them the louder they became. I personally like to call that "something," God.

I lost so many close friends to drugs and who were murdered. This lifestyle wasn't fun anymore. It seemed like I was going from one funeral to another. It seemed like someone was getting killed every week.

It also seemed like someone was always having a house party – music, drinking and drugs. At one house party, the drinks were in the kitchen. I was drinking dark rum as if it were water. I was refilling before I finished the cup I no longer cared about the party. I stayed in the kitchen, downing one cup after another. I have no idea how many cups I had, but people started taking it way from me. I remember people telling my friend to take me home. I could barely stand up. Everything started to feel like a dream. I didn't feel conscious. I kept telling myself to snap out of it. I was only a few blocks from home, but a friend had to drive – I couldn't walk. She propped me up against the door, rang the doorbell and took off before my mom opened it. As soon as the door opened, I fell in and crawled. I couldn't even pretend. I was losing control of my bodily functions. I felt like life was seeping out of me. I could barely hold my head up. If numb was what I was aiming for, I was there. I fell down and couldn't feel anything. I had been drunk many times before, but this was different. I wasn't just drunk, I was alcohol poisoned. My heart was beating very slowly and I had a horrible taste in my mouth that I had never tasted before. I felt like I was one cup away from dying. I think this was the first time in a very long time that I prayed. I sensed that I was dying at the age of seventeen.

I had never felt that way before. I was sick for about a week with cold sweats, hot flashes, and slobbering uncontrollably. I cried, "God please save me." I finally realized that I wanted to live. I kept telling myself to stay up. I guess God heard me. My body started rejecting the alcohol and detoxing. I kept a small garbage can on side of the bed. For days, I had a severe case of diarrhea and vomiting. I still can see and feel the hurt and disappointment on my mother's face.

Days had gone by and I was still so sick. I had no energy. If the TV was on, I couldn't get up to change a channel. I was wrapped up, layers of clothes with a hood on. A show called "AM Chicago" came on, and the host of the show was Oprah Winfrey. I don't remember the episode, but I do remember she was crying and talking about some of the things she had been through, like being molested. I watched her all week. I thought, wow; look at all she's been through – maybe there's hope for me. I would rush home from school to watch the show.

I did not drink for almost a month. I never wanted to feel that way again. But I did not stop drinking right away; I was just more cautious about how much I drank. During this one year, there were so many things that were happening that my soul felt like it was being revived. My outlook on life was slowly changing.

One day, I was drinking with a group of friends near my grandmother's house. A friend of mine named Tom, started talking about goals and dreams. I was a little tipsy, but I did not want to talk about dreams and goals. I just wanted to be mellowed out. He asked, "Where do you see yourself in five years?" He talked about changing his life for the betterment of himself and his son. He did not want that type of lifestyle for his son. My soul was listening even though I did not want to.

Two weeks later, we went to a school-related event. We would always go as a group. Tom did not go because he was on the path of turning his life around. Well, a fight broke out. Tom had a reputation for being a good fighter. So someone went to get him. He fought the guy and won, but as soon as he was getting up, the guy shot him in the chest. I heard the gunshots and someone yelled, "Tom got shot!" We all ran over. A mutual friend had him in his arms, rocking him. I looked at Tom and we made eye contact. Tears were rolling down his cheek. I felt it. The ambulance was taking forever to come.

Tom looked at me as if he knew he wasn't going to make it. When the ambulance took him away, I lost it. Someone grabbed me and I just broke down. I could barely walk. Then I went numb and in shock. I couldn't stop thinking about everything Tom had been saying to my sister and me on my grandmother's front steps. In the hospital emergency room, there were so many people that the hospital told everyone to leave for security reasons. So we waited in someone's driveway, some people were just sitting on the grass, waiting to hear word, in complete silence. Someone walked up and told us the news that they tried to revive Tom, but he was dead on arrival. I was so numb I couldn't think, couldn't feel.

After about a week or two of just moping around the house, I couldn't get the thoughts out of my head of Tom saying, I want more out of life. I kept thinking about the question he asked, "Where do you see yourself five years from now?" I had never thought about it. I had no idea where I wanted to be in five years. I had never thought about what I wanted out of life.

I started to look at where the path I was on would lead me. The way I looked at life started to gradually change. Things I use to do that made sense at one time, no longer made sense and started to lose their appeal. I was beginning to have a conscience about what I was doing to myself. My soul had been dormant for so long, but it was beginning to wake up. I couldn't even answer a simple question: Who am I? What is the purpose of my existence? There had to be more to life than this.

LOST

We turn to God for help when our foundations are shaking, only to learn that it is God who is shaking them.

- C. C. West

THE DAY MY SOUL CRIED

LOST

There were so many people in my life who tried to reach out to me, like my mother, grandmother, neighbors, and even a few friends. But I had to see it for myself. Well, my mom and grandmother reached out with a belt first, then there were talks, but they did *reach out* to me. They probably thought I wasn't listening, but subconsciously I heard every word.

I had no idea how or where to start, but I wanted so much more out of life. I thought: okay, I'll go to college and get a decent job, not realizing until then how I had limited my choices. I had a bad track record: Juvenile detention, carrying a "D" average, graduating a year later than I was supposed to, caught stealing and taken to jail. And I could barely read. *How was I supposed to fix this?*

I started surrounding myself with positive things. I started going back to church with my mother and grandmother.

But still I was so lost. Have you ever spent the night at someone's house and slept so well that when you woke up, for a split second you had no idea where you were? That's how I felt. My *soul* had been asleep for so long. I had people around me, but I felt alone and empty. I needed to find God and myself. I needed to figure out who am I? What do I want out of life? Where do I go from here?

I decided to go to college. So, I went to the alternative school I had just graduated from to talk with a counselor to figure out my options. She looked at me like I was speaking a foreign language. I guess, based on my transcripts and past, she assumed she was wasting her time. She wasn't the only one that did not take me seriously. When I told people I wanted to go to college, for some reason this was a joke. How could I have expected anything else? All they could base their image of me on was my previous behavior, which had proven that this wasn't something I would remotely be interested in or stick with. Now if it had been a year or two earlier, I would have been discouraged by the negative responses, but it wasn't about them or what anyone thought anymore.

After asking several people, someone eventually told me about a local community college. I went to talk to the admission representative about what my options were. I had never taken the SAT (Scholastic Aptitude Test), entrance exams, or any college prep classes. She told me that I had to take a basic academic entrance exam. All I had to do was pass this test. She assured me that it was very easy. I was hopeful. She further informed me that they only gave the test once and if I wanted to start in June, I would have to take the test in May. I could not wait to start school.

What major was I going to take? I starred at the degree programs and looked at the classes and was confused. I had no idea about what I wanted to do. So, I decided to get a certificate in Word Processing. I wanted to be able to get a "good" paying job. Okay, now I have a plan. I would be twenty when I get my certificate.

It was time to take the test. There was a group of us in the conference room at a round table. Once we were done with the test, we had to put our pencils down, turn in our test, and wait for everyone else to finish. I think I was only halfway through when everyone was waiting on me to finish. I was overwhelmed. What was I thinking? I had no idea what the answers were. So, I started guessing. It all looked foreign. Finally, the test papers were collected.

Everyone passed but me. I was devastated and broke down crying. Well, I did more than cry, I snapped, as if it were their fault that I failed. I was so embarrassed, but this time it was different. I didn't want to escape; I wanted to go to school. I need this! I want this! I refuse to believe that this is it for me. I cried and would not leave the room. The admissions rep pulled me to the side; she knew how bad I wanted it. I had been bugging her for weeks, and she knew how excited and hopeful I was. For the first time in my life I was looking forward to my future. So, she offered to give me the answers. I took the paper, but it crossed my mind that I couldn't do it. I thought if I cheat on this test, I will have to continue to cheat my way through school. I called her later and said, "Please just tell me what areas I need to study." She was impressed that I wanted to do it for myself. It was so much more than just an entry exam to me. I did not want to fail anymore. I did not want to give up.

Many people had counted me out and given up on me. I was told that I wouldn't become anything in life. Usually, I would believe them, but not this time. I was so determined.

My mother and I got some books and sat on my grandmother's porch for a few days as I studied. The rep from the college told me that I could come back in 30 days to retake the test. I was gradually walking away from my wild lifestyle. I did not party or drink. I stayed in the house studying every day. I wanted to pass this test so badly. When I went back and took the test I passed it. I was a few points away from failing it again, but I didn't fail. I passed! I started school in July 1991.

When I first started, my grades were low. I studied day in day out. I would often fall asleep with my books in the bed. I tried different methods and eventually, I learned a method that worked. I read everything I could get my hands on – newspaper and magazines with a dictionary in one hand. Every word I was stuck on I looked up in the dictionary. I got books on vocabulary and English and studied constantly.

I maintained a C average. Right before it was time for me to graduate and get my certificate, I learned I was pregnant. The father and I didn't have an *official* relationship; I guess you can say we were acquaintances with *benefits*. At first, I was not happy when I learned I was pregnant. I thought about all the things that I was trying to accomplish. I thought this was not the right *time* for me to be having a child. I entertained the thought of having an abortion. I couldn't sleep and on my way to the clinic made a u-turn to the shopping mall to get maternity clothes. It will never be the right time. I had to own up to my responsibilities of being a young parent with or without his father. I have no regrets. My son has been a blessing. I took time off after my son was born. I was now a single parent; I worked part-time and went to school fulltime.

My son Zyair was born with a severe case of clubfeet, a birth defect. He was in a cast when he was two weeks old. His feet were shaped like golf clubs. One foot was more severe than the other – his heel was connected to his calf. The muscles were so tight in his foot that it looked like a balled up fist. The first pediatric foot surgeon I took him to was very negative. He would tell me with pity in his eyes, "Oh, you.re such a strong single mom. I will try my best to correct his foot, but I've never seen or worked on a case this severe." Every time I left his office, I was in tears. He said he needed to do emergency surgery on Zyair so I asked him to help me get a second opinion. I was not comfortable with him cutting on my baby and he had doubt in his own work. He had doubts that my son would ever walk. I never went back to him.

The foot surgeon he sent me to for a second opinion was so positive, and he assured me that Zyair's foot could be fixed. He assured me that not only would my son walk, but he was confident he would be running and playing sports. Of course, he had to tell me the downside too but he was very confident in his work and he was a man of faith. He's the one! Zyair had the surgery when he was four months old and then again at nine months. I spent a lot of time in the hospital. But just like the doctor said, he was not only walking before he was one year old, he was running. This experience opened my eyes to *possibility.*

One day my mom asked me to go to church with her. I had Zyair on my lap and I was so overwhelmed with emotion. I saw the look in my mom's eyes as she smiled, looking at me and my son. When the pastor did an altar call, Zyair, who was about two years old then, walked up to the altar to be prayed for. When we returned to our seat, my mother had tears in her eyes as she reached out to me. I got choked up and started to cry. As we hugged, I whispered in her ear, "All the hurt and pain I.ve ever caused you, I am so sorry. Please forgive me, I love you, Ma." I thought about not just the pain I had caused her, but all she had endured. I think being a mother made me see her pain from a different perspective.

After all the surgeries were over with, I went back to school and received my Associate degree in Accounting in 1993. I continued until I received my second Associate degree in Business Management in

1995. During the last two years of school, I was an "A" and "B" average student.

I still wasn't sure exactly what I wanted to do, but I knew I wanted my own business. I knew I wanted to make a difference in the world. But I had no idea what that would be. I was just getting to know me. I was still in search of God's purpose for my life.

THE DAY MY SOUL CRIED

THE HEALING BEGINS

When you hold resentment toward another, you are bound to that person or condition by an emotional link that is stronger than steel. Forgiveness is the only way to dissolve that link and get free.

– C. Ponder

THE DAY MY SOUL CRIED

THE HEALING BEGINS

My mom and I began to get very close. I was also very close to my grandmother. Now I could talk to them both about anything. I was about 21 or 22 years old when, one day, my mom came home and said, "We.re quitting smoking," and held up a roll of suckers. At the time, I was trying to lose weight and thought okay, I need to quit smoking, too. I went cold turkey on everything – sexual activities, drinking, smoking, and going out, EVERYTHING. I was going to church, praying, being a good mom, and working.

I was trying to put my values and morals into perspective. I asked myself: What is important to me? How could I become a better mother, daughter, sister – a better me?

I thought if I do the right thing and focus on today and my future, my past would fade away. Although on the outside, I appeared to be different, I was walking the walk, trying to talk the talk, but I was still hurting. I could not figure out why, after doing everything right, why I was still in pain. I would often hear the pastor say, just give it to God and He'll take care of it. But I had no idea what I was holding on to. If I don't understand why I feel so empty, how could I give it to God? What am I giving Him? I often prayed for God to just show me what He needed for me to see. Just show me what I need to let go of. Just show me what you need from me.

Okay, when I was giving everything up, food became the replacement for everything. While I was shoving everything out of my life, I was shoving food into my mouth. Instead of drinking myself numb, I was eating until I couldn't move. It got very bad. I would go to three different fast food restaurants, purchasing full meals, just for lunch. I would have a foot-long, sub-sandwich and bag of chips from one place, a hamburger, fries, and soda from another place and a strawberry shake from another. Then, I'd sit and eat it all in one serving. You'd better not ask me to share. I got sick of people watching me eat or asking, "You.re going to eat all of that?" But I had no shame. My excuse was I only eat like this once a day. I gained almost 100 pounds in one year. I didn't even realize I had gained that much weight. Everyone tried to tell me I needed to lose weight. I thought they were "tripping" and I wasn't that big. My grandmother said to me, "Baby, you don't have to eat the whole chicken, just eat a piece and push away from the table." My mom said, Yvonne, you.re a pretty girl; you just don't look like yourself and I'm concerned." My sister said, with pity in her eyes, "Girl, the type of guy you.re attracted to likes a fit type of woman. You've got to get the weight off." My response was, as I gasped for breath, "If a guy don't love me for me, I don't need to be with him." I was in serious denial. You would think going from a size 11-12 to a 20-something and having to purchase a triple X-large would have given me a clue.

I did not even realize that I stopped looking in the mirror, kept the house dark, and hated to leave the house unless I had too. I was suffering in silence. Well, I thought it was in silence, but apparently not because people would always ask, "Are you okay?" I gradually started to pick up some of my old habits – drinking, cursing like a sailor, and smoking cigarettes.

Everyone tried to intervene, but I did not see myself as overweight, until I saw a photograph. I had gone to California to spend some time with my dad's side of the family – Grandma Vonn, Auntie Shelia, and cousins. We took lots of pictures. When I returned home and developed the pictures, I had no idea who that girl was in the photos. Oh my God, it was me! I saw myself for the first time overweight.

I started working in the kitchen at a casino boat in Gary, Indiana as a Stuart (dish washer). I took the job because I was told that all the office positions were filled and when one opened up, they would consider me. I had two degrees, but no experience. So, I took the job to get my foot in the door. I went to Human Resources (HR) every few weeks to ask if there were any positions available. Although I saw new people starting in these positions, every time I went to talk to HR I was told "that position was just filled. Be patient, we haven't forgotten about you." When I asked about the new employees, I was told that they had experience. Okay, I realized there was a very slim chance that I was going to get an office position anytime soon. But I couldn't afford to just quit; I needed to plan to move on.

There was another girl who I worked with and we often talked to about goals and dreams. And we talked about losing weight. Then, we decided to become walking partners. We worked midnights, from 10:00 p.m. until 6:00 a.m. After work we would go to the running track in the morning and motivate each other to eat right. Working in the kitchen was a lot of exercise and movement, so I looked at it as an additional daily workout. That helped me cope with having to stick around longer. I did not like how the chef, the cooks, the waiters, and even the busboys, looked at us like we were worthless. This was very humbling. I don't care how much money you make or what "title" you hold, you don't treat people like that. I would get so mad. I would voice my opinion, but I took my anger out on the track. I looked at it as a workout and tried to make work fun.

I began to only eat salads and healthy food. We gradually increased the laps we did around the track. There was a high bridge in the area and on one side of that bridge was a long flight of stairs down to the street.

We started running the stairs and walking back and forth over the bridge. We would park far away so that we could walk to the bridge. During our walks we would talk about our dreams and goals. I lost about 60+ pounds in about six months. It felt like it melted off.

During this time my sister and I lived together and we would alternate taking care of the kids because she worked during the day and I worked at night. This worked out well because I could sleep while the kids where at school.

At the time, I was about 23 years old. I had a girl's doll that I invented. She was a life-size, talking African-American doll with a remote controlled walker. This was my dream. My life revolved around this project. But I had no idea how or what to do. So, I contacted an invention submission company based in Chicago to take it to, but I needed a ride. So, I contacted an old friend to drive me and I offered to pay him for his time. He knew his way around Chicago. He was also someone I once dated, but now I was repulsed by the thought of having sex with him. I only saw him as a friend. He came and took me to my appointment. When we got back, my sister left for work. I was trying to be nice, but I wanted him to leave. The kids were in the living room with their backs toward the kitchen. The place was a duplex and we used the side door more often than the front door, which was in the kitchen. There was a pantry door with a glass panel and you had to go through the pantry to get to the side door. The kids' eyes were glued to the TV. I gave my "friend" the money for taking me, said thank you and started to walk him to the door. He refused to take the money and said, "You look good, Yvonne." I thanked him as I opened the door. He closed it. With confusion on my face, I asked him, "What are you doing?" I thought he was crazy – kids were right there. He overpowered me. I was going to fight, but I looked at the kids where were about three or four years old at the time and stopped fighting. I did not want them to turn around and see that. The tears were streaming down my face. I was praying, God please don't let them turn around, and begging, him to stop at the same time.

When he left, I locked the door. I made sure the kids were occupied, and tried to hold it together as I went upstairs to get into the tub. I ran the water hot as I can stand it and scrubbed my skin over and over and over as I cried. Again, I thought, I brought this on myself. This was my fault. I shouldn't have asked him to take me. Maybe I shouldn't make myself look attractive.

I wanted to live in a different state. I gave my job a deadline as to when they had to offer me an office position. If not, I wanted to leave. Just driving down the streets was painful for me. Many of my friends were dead, in jail, or strung out on drugs. There were too many memories of who I was and no longer wanted to be. I just wanted to go. I started drinking again, although not as bad as before.

My sister and I put our tax refund checks together and moved to metro Atlanta in 1998. I had never been to Atlanta, but I thought this was the fresh new start that I needed. My sister had lived there before, so she thought I should see if I liked it. We visited for a week and I loved it. I went home, gave the place where I worked a two week notice and started packing. We drove to Atlanta and I have been here every since. I still go home to see family, but for the most part my mom and grandmother come to visit. About a year after we moved, our Mom and my brother eventually moved to Atlanta, too.

I wasn't looking for a relationship. My mission was to move to Atlanta to chase my dreams. I had been told that Atlanta was a Mecca for African American businesses and I believed that my chances for success would be greater. Love was the last thing on my mind. I had in my head that it was just going to be me and Zyair. Marriage wasn't on my list of objectives.

But, I met Steffan a few months after moving to Atlanta. I had to go to work the next morning but I just did not want to hang-up the phone. We talked and laughed for hours and I lost track of time. The sun was rising. It was about 5:00 a.m. and I needed to be at work at 8:00 a.m. I worked in the accounting department of a company, so I had to be sharp in the morning, in fact all day. I yawned and stretched for hours. I dozed off and my head almost hit the desk. I jumped up and went outside for a smoke. I used every way to talk negatively about relationships and that I wasn't here looking for love. My co-worker followed me and gave me the look.

"You didn't get much sleep last night did ya? You met someone, didn't you?"

"It wasn't like that at all," I said, laughing. I told her I met this guy and we were up all night on the phone as I smiled.

Weeks went by and she would always look at me with her lip turned up and a smirk on her face, "Aha, you.re falling in love!" "No, I'm not, we.re just friends," I said, trying to keep a straight face. She was right. I was falling in love, but fighting it. Eventually, Steffan and I moved in together.

I was still pushing for the doll invention that I believed in so much. I had been paying this invention submission company for years to take care of it all for me, but after so long I took it into my own hands. I could not allow love to interfere with my focus. I submitted it to all the shopping networks and a large well-known toy manufacturer. They both rejected me. This sent me into a deep depression. I gained all my weight back and I pushed Steffan out of my life. It was easier for me to let go and run. As always, I was still subconsciously pushing people out of my life, thinking it would prevent me from getting hurt. After two years of living together, Steffan got fed up and moved out.

I began sinking deeper into depression. I bought every motivational book and tape I could get my hands on to pull myself out of it. It had gotten so bad that just getting out the bed was hard. I was not just dealing with the breakup; I needed to deal with my past. However, I needed closure from the relationship, so I wrote him this poem:

CLOSURE

We started out as friends, you and me
We fell in love, it was destined to be
Over the years things changed so dramatically
Our final words ended so suddenly
It was hard for me, because I thought at least
friends we would be
At first I took it personally
Everything happens for a reason, you see
I never knew love till you and me

I guess I never thought this would be, a growing
pain for me
Time and things do change even what I thought
was meant to be
The best thing is now I am starting to know and
love me
You have served your purpose with me
Saying this is closure for me
And now it's time for me to totally set you free

I needed to heal. How do you heal and how do
you let the past go? I was so busy running from pain I
never gave myself a chance to face it. I thought that
walking the walk, thinking positive, and having a new
start was the answer. I was wrong. I was still suffering
in silence. What all was I holding on to? Why couldn't I
let it go? I don't understand why I am STILL in so much
pain, I kept thinking.

I prayed for God to take it all away, but I needed
to deal with it head on. I needed to forgive those who
had hurt me. I needed to come to some type of
understanding. I needed to truly let go. I used to tell

Steffan about my past over and over and over. Although I had moved away and had this positive outlook on life, I was still living in the past. I carried it around with me like invisible luggage. Although no one, not even me, could see it, it was weighing on me. I was moving forward in life, but I was also walking backwards. I was accomplishing things and seeing new surroundings but I was still focused on my past.

I was about 29 years old at the time. When I thought about all the goals I wanted to accomplish by this age and realized I wasn't even close, I started to cry. Why me? God, what did I do to deserve so much pain? I fell asleep as the tears were falling down my face. I prayed so hard that night.

That night I dreamed about it. I was being attacked by some type of demons and monsters. I used to have recurring nightmares as a kid about monsters attacking me and I mastered how to wake myself up.

The dream...

I was running in a panic trying hard wake myself up. It wasn't working. Somehow, I got hold of a phone and tried to call everyone I knew. But it was like no one can hear me. No matter how loud I shouted no one could hear me. So, I continued to try to escape. An image of an angel, I couldn't see her face, stopped me, pointed toward the demons and told me to go back. I laughed and said, "With all due respect, I refuse to go back." I said, "Why would you want me to go back and fight? They are stronger than me. I'm powerless." She said, "You are as powerless as you believe you are. You have to have faith that God is there. He is within you, but you have to believe. Now go back and fight without fear. Trust that you'll win." I thought, why can't God fight them off for me; why do I have to fight them? She must have heard me because she said, "God can't do it for you, you have to do it for yourself and trust that he's right there to protect you. But it is something you much do." I felt so powerful. I went back with a vengeance and started to fight.

I woke up.

I was driving and listening to the radio and a song by Elton John called, "I'm Still Standing." I thought, after all I.ve been through, I'm still standing! I cannot begin to heal until I come to some type of peace.

My past didn't break me. I then decided to face my past and pull strength from it. I had to understand that there were some things that I had absolutely no control over; I had to forgive in order to move forward. I gradually started taking off the weight. I was beginning to let it go and realize that I made it through all that. I went through a long process of forgiveness and healing, which comes from understanding. Those who hurt me were wounded themselves. The world is not against me. I am not a victim, I'm a victor. I survived it. Now it's time to let it go. The fact is those things happened, and I cannot change what happened, but I can change the way I look at it. I thought forgiveness was for those who hurt me. I thought by forgiving I was giving them the okay for what they did. No, that did not mean I now had to befriend them. I don't have to ever speak to them again, but I did not want to carry the bitterness in my heart. You see, forgiving them was for me, for my peace of mind, not theirs.

I started working out again and I joined a dance team. No, I wasn't trying to be a professional dancer; it was for weight loss and to help me overcome my fears. I decided to do things that I enjoyed. I began to look at life so much more clearly. I began to pull it all together. I needed that time alone. I needed God to put me in a place where all I could do is look up and look within. I needed those times of reflecting. I have heard several times that you shouldn't look back. I agree that you cannot stay there, but there are lesson we have to learn from our past.

Steffan and I were separated for a year, but we were still friends. Eventually, we started dating again.

I was pregnant with his first and my second child. I was not happy at first; I was thinking, I finally got the weight off, now I'm about to gain weight again. But after the first time I felt movement, I loved my unborn. Steffan went to every appointment, every ultrasound, and every late night trip to get me some French fries. We found out it was going to be a boy. Zyon was born five weeks early and he was diagnosed with Down syndrome right after birth. Both my sons have had a huge positive impact on my life. There are so many life lessons I.ve learned through them. I.ve learned so much more about myself. I had come a long way, but I still had a way to go.

MY SOUL CRIED

If you aren't good at loving yourself, you will have a difficult time loving anyone, since you'll resent the time and energy you give another person that you aren't even giving to yourself.

- B. De Angelis

THE DAY MY SOUL CRIED

MY SOUL CRIED

We were doing okay. Steffan and I were both working. Zyair was doing well in school. Zyon was almost two years old and doing great in therapy. He was starting to walk. They both went to the same daycare. Zyair went there before and after school; he was in elementary school.

Then things started to have a snowball effect. Steffan lost his job. I signed up for public assistance to help with child care. After receiving assistance for about six months, I had to meet with my caseworker and she informed me that they had changed the amount you could earn in order to receive public assistance. I made $2,000 too much annually. I just looked at the case worker and started to cry. There was no way we could afford childcare and we were barely getting by. Daycare was about $150 per week, just for Zyon. Heck, all I brought home was about $300 a week. Necessities alone – rent, utilities, car insurance, food – left us about two hundred dollars short every month, and that was without child care costs.

I was asked to speak at a women's and children's homeless shelter. I had put together a guided journal which included by life story and I had about 100 of them printed; I donated most of them to the shelter. It was called "Phoqus" (pronounced focus). It consisted of two books – one represented the past, which is where I tell my story and the reader was to then write their story. The second book represented the future, a 12-month journal focusing on your goals. Great concept but I had no idea about publishing or writing, which is a story in itself. Anyway, I was prepared to give a five-minute speech thinking there would be other guest speakers. Well, the night before I was told that I was the ONLY speaker. OMG, I panicked. What was I going to say to these women? I had struggled most of my life, but I had never been homeless. I wasn't prepared, but I stayed up all night looking for resources to help them get back on their feet. I prayed for God to use me as a vessel, because I had no idea what I was going to say to them. Who was I to tell them how to cope with being homeless or how to overcome it if I.ve never been there myself? I couldn't fully relate. That was probably the toughest crowd I'll ever face to motivate, but surprisingly, it went really well.

The day before Thanksgiving, Steffan had an extra day off from work and the kids were home from school. But I had to work that day. As soon as I got to my desk, Steffan called me. We were being evicted. I told my boss what was going on and that I needed to leave immediately. I was on the phone with the property manager as I was driving home. I was very upset. They told me we had until December 14th to get caught up. I questioned why I was being evicted after I had been told that we had time.

Steffan and the kids were asleep. Steffan heard someone coming into the house while ringing the doorbell. When he reached the top of the staircase the Sherriff was coming up the stairs. All they had on was their pajamas. When I arrived at home, I went straight to the Sherriff demanding that he stop the guys from throwing my things out.

It felt surreal. I stood there looking around. I looked at my children and all of a sudden I had this sense of peace. I had to get it together and think clearly for them. I went into survival mode. I scrambled through our things already thrown outside to find the kids' clothes, shoes and coats to put on. It was cold outside. We had been saving up to pay the rent, so I handed Steffan the money and told him to get a moving truck. My oldest son, who was about 12 years old at the time, was confused; he thought we were being robbed. We had never been evicted before. After I calmed him down, I sent him back to watch possessions. I had to find Zyon's stroller – we had to shoo people away. They were jumping out of their cars and pulling up like it was a garage sale. I was amazed at how bold people were walking up to me and saying things like, "Ma'am, I'm sorry about what happened to you but can I have that TV?" Wow! I began to sort through the things. I made two piles. One was of those things that were important or that we would need, and the other pile were things people could grab. I explained to my son that these were just things and they could be replaced. We put our things in storage and rode around for hours looking for a hotel to stay in.

We could have stayed with my mom who had a small, one-bedroom apartment, Steffan and I agreed that we needed to learn to pull ourselves out of this. How were we going to learn if we looked for others to save us?

In three months we got back on our feet and moved into an apartment.

My mom came over one day and said, "Yvonne, are you okay?" Why did this sound familiar? Why does everyone keep asking me that? Nothing is wrong, I'm fine, I thought.

I used to care about how I looked. I was too cheap to pay a hairdresser, but kept my hair done. I tried to manage my weight, and was picky about the clothing I wore. I was a neat freak. I wanted my home to look and smell good all the time. My mom noticed that I was letting everything, including myself, go, but I didn't see it.

It was about 8:00 a.m. one morning. It was beautiful day outside. I was looking at the trees and enjoying the breeze. The kids were off to school and Steffan was leaving for work. I grabbed a cup of coffee and a cigarette and was standing on the porch. It was if something clicked in my mind and my eyes opened like never before. I looked into the house from outside. I opened the door and I walked through my home as if I was touring it, seeing it for the first time. I went to the bathroom and looked in the mirror. My hair was a hot mess. My clothes were ragged. I did not even realize that I had stopped looking at myself in the mirror for years. I would look just enough to do my hair. My nails were chipped. My skin looked bad. I had gained weight.

I looked in the mirror and stared at myself as if I was looking at someone else. Oh, my soul cried out. Oh my God, what am I doing? What have I done? I fell to my knees. I wasn't living in the reality of the world I had created around myself. It wasn't until that moment that I realized why I was sabotaging my success and making myself look undesirable. It wasn't until that moment; I realized I was standing in my own way. I had created this fictitious life of joy, but I wasn't being realistic with myself. Yes, I thought positive about everyone else, but I was mentally abusing myself. When I stood in the mirror, my first thoughts were: you.re so ugly. Others no longer had the power to hurt me; I was hurting myself. I wanted to be undesirable because I did not like the feeling of being a "piece of meat." I did not want to be sexually abused again so I made myself undesirable. No matter how much Steffan told me he loved me, I did not believe him, because I didn't love myself. I was always looking for reasons why he was with me. He's only with me because of the kids, I thought. He's only with me because I'm convenient. I never once thought he was with me because he genuinely loved me. I never believed the good things people would say about me; I always thought there was an ulterior motive behind it.

OMG, I.ve forgiven and let go of everything in my past, I told myself. I.ve changed the way I see the world. But I never changed the way I saw myself. I never forgave myself. I cried for weeks. This wasn't your typical cry. It literally felt like the walls of my chest opened up and my soul was screaming.

THE DAY MY SOUL CRIED

UNBROKEN

Confront the dark parts of yourself, and work to banish them with illumination and forgiveness. Your willingness to wrestle with your demons will cause your angels to sing. Use the pain as fuel, as a reminder of your strength.

– A. Wilson

THE DAY MY SOUL CRIED

UNBROKEN

I know you've heard it a million times, but it's a fact: *Perception and attitude are* EVERYTHING! The difference between how I face life now versus when I was younger is perception. I have come to understand that hardship, hurt, and pain does not discriminate. Its how it is dealt with that makes the difference. I don't watch sports on TV much, but one day I was watching a boxing match between Leila Ali and another boxer. Leila walked into the ring with confidence and one of her strategies, which was what her dad used as well, was to get inside the opponent's head. Before the match she put so much fear and doubt in this woman that I realized she had defeated her before they even entered the ring! Ali was prepared; she came out with confidence that this woman was not going to beat her. When her opponent came out, her head was down and you could see the fear in her eyes. Ali had this confident attitude – like you might get a few good hits, you might even knock me down, but I'll win. The woman couldn't even look Ali in the eye. When the bell rang for the fight to start, I could tell the woman did not even try to put up a good fight, because she walked into the ring already defeated.

Our thoughts of ourselves and our attitude determine our ability to endure and eventually overcome. I know now that strength is a mind state, not something that a select few possess. The difference between when I was a little girl struggling to read and now a postgraduate student was my perception of the obstacle and my determination and confidence that I could conquer it. Then, I thought it was impossible and farfetched dreams so I didn't even try. We were built to endure it is one of those things we tell ourselves without even realizing that's what makes it hard for us to endure.

Obstacles helped me develop my passion; my passion is where my purpose lives.

I read this quote a whole back: "The problem is not that there are problems. The problem is expecting otherwise and thinking that having problems is a problem."

I know life is going to throw things my way. I still fall to my knees crying out to God when storms come my way. I am learning more and more to trust Him. To trust that with God I can get through it. I choose to be unbroken!

BREATHE

Sketch by Jeffrey R. Miller

THE DAY MY SOUL CRIED

BREATHE by Yvonne N. Pierre

At first, it's hard to understand why life has to be

such a maturing pain for you to seek

and endure what life has to offer, so to speak.

They say experience is our best instructor, listen

closely, don't dare sleep

'cause when times get rough you'll need

to reflect back on how you seemed

To conquer the hurt and pain that had you feeling

like, "I can't breathe!"

Some were created and some were simply meant to
be.

Don't get caught up on the "Why Me's?"

You need to understand step two before you advance
to step three.

Anger and anxiety makes it hard to focus and

make the right decisions.

Life is a learning process, don't you dare cheat.

Every moment is a small puzzle piece to a much
greater purpose only God can see.

Learn all you can, be observant and remove the
option of defeated.

Use your past experiences to make you stronger, not
beaten.

Don't allow your pain to be a roadblock, but you've
got wings

to fly over, push through and stay on the path that

you are destined to achieve.

What you.re going through is a test that you

MUST achieve,

just move out of your own way, inhale, you'll

pass, just don't forget to breathe!

ABOUT THE AUTHOR

Yvonne N. Pierre is a devoted mom of two boys, ages 17 and 8. Before becoming a mother, Yvonne always had a passion for developing works in the entertainment  industry - film, books, and projects - that empower others. After her youngest son was born and was diagnosed with Down syndrome, she redirected her attention and primary efforts toward the special needs community. She is in the process of developing new projects that will empower the special needs community here and abroad. Yvonne is the founder of Have Ya Heard (HYH), an online community and e-magazine whose primary focus is to highlights the accomplishments of those with special needs. She is the founder of a publishing company, Zyonair's Unlimited, LLC named after her two sons.

In addition, Yvonne is also a radio personality on her own show – The Yvonne Pierre Show hosted on BlogTalkRadio. It's an on-demand talk radio show dedicated to informing and inspiring listeners on topics ranging from self-improvement to parenting a special needs child.

Connect with Yvonne via the web on:

Facebook: http://www.facebook.com/ypierre01

Twitter: http://www.twitter.com/ypierre

MySpace: http://www.myspace.com/hyhonline

Website: http://www.zyonair.com

CPSIA information can be obtained at www.ICGtesting.com
Printed in the USA
BVOW011612080713

325352BV00011B/648/P